The Best So

Tasty and Healthy 　　　　*μ υσ jυι ιου*

and Your Family

Table of Contents

Introduction

Having a fast-paced life in the 21st century has direct effects on every person's diet. Being constantly on the go and catching up on the daily rigors of life makes a majority of people forget the importance of proper nutrition and good health. This is not an isolated situation; this is becoming the new normal for people all over the world.

The direct effect of not having enough time is not being able to prepare a well-thought of, balanced diet for oneself and the family. Everything served on the table is more often fried or just bought from fast food chains. This trend should not continue if the goal is to live a healthy, prosperous life.

Why then make a cookbook filled with recipes for soups? Think about it. When one eats out and has the time and the budget to really have a full meal, doesn't it start with a warm, sumptuous soup dish? Soups are served at the beginning of important meals for many reasons. One, a warm bowl of soup provides hungry patrons with enough nutrients to quiet down rumbling stomachs. Second, a hearty serving of soup provides good enough nutrients that are good for the body. Third, soup consumed before the main course will prevent people from overeating. Lastly, soups can warm up the body which wakes up the digestive system.

There are many health benefits connected to consuming soups and this is not just believed by one culture. Have a trip around the world and see the many cultures that serve soup not just to satisfy one's palate but to bring in loads of nutrients to the body. Go to Asia and discover the Japanese miso soup which is believed to have anti-cancer and anti-virus properties. Fly to Eastern Europe and discover the famous Polish Split Pea Soup which is believed to have enough dietary fibers that prevent cardiovascular diseases. Or have a trip to North America and taste the famous Chicken Soup given to fever-stricken persons.

All around the world, soup has been the go-to dish for people with illnesses, people who aim to lose weight, and people who want to be healthy. So why not make a cookbook full of good, sumptuous recipes for soups? Soup must be a staple in everyone's dining tables and hopefully, this book will help bring back soup's glory days.

There should be no excuse for having no time to prepare a soup dish. Soups are very easy to cook and are not so taxing especially for newbies. This is why the book is divided into several sections – each section dedicated to a method of preparing a soup. The first section focuses on traditional soups from various cultures. In this section, one can expect to learn the preparation of a creamy soup and the preparation of a clear soup. There are also some tomato based soup recipes as well as vegetable based soup recipes. The second section focuses on the use of a pressure cooker. Pressure cookers have been used in the kitchen for centuries to tenderize meat with the shorter amount of time. This section of the book will introduce more hearty soups – soups with the inclusion of root crops or meat. The third section of the book highlights the reliability of a slow cooker. This section is dedicated to those with little time to prepare healthy enough dishes for the family. Slow cookers are easy to use; just put all the ingredients, set it to the correct heat level, set the timer, and expect a good soup dish after a few hours. Also in the book you will find vegetarian-friendly soup recipes. Ideal for vegetarians and for the health-conscious, that have little time to spare in the kitchen.

Try all the recipes in this book and see what you have been missing all this time. Soups should be a part of each and everyone's menu not just as an added dish on the dinner table but as a supplement to everyone's dietary needs. Keep your tummies full, healthy, and clean by consuming a serving of good, sumptuous soup before taking your main course. You will see the difference in your body after just a few days of changing your diet.

Wanton Soup

(Ready in 40 minutes with 35 minutes prep time- serves 4)

Ingredients:

- 1 wonton filling

- 2 cans (400g each) chicken broth with reduced sodium

- Corse salt to taste

- 3 thinly sliced scallions

- 3 teaspoons rice vinegar

- ½ teaspoon toasted sesame oil

Cooking directions:

1. In a large bowl, make the soup by combining 4 cups of water, the salt, and broth.

2. Bring to boil

3. The wantons should be added one at a time and allow to boil again

4. When all the wontons are in, reduce the heat and cook the wantons slowly until they are cooked. This should take about 6 minutes.

5. Stir in the sesame oil, salt, vinegar, and sesame oil.

6. Serve the soup

Thai Chicken & Vegetable Soup
(Ready in 45 minutes with 30 minutes preparation time- serves 5)

Ingredients:

- ½ cup of carrots sliced into matchstick like stripes

- 1 tablespoon coconut oil

- 11/2 cups red pepper, cubed

- 1 cup sliced mushrooms

- 2 cups chicken broth

- 2 tablespoons of ginger root, peeled and minced

- 1/4teaspoon of cayenne pepper

- 2 tablespoons lemon juice

- 14 ounces (1 can) coconut milk, unsweetened

- 2 cups cubed chicken breast, boneless

- 2 teaspoon grated lime zest

- 11/2 teaspoon lemon zest, grated

- 2 tablespoon fresh cilantro, chopped

Cooking directions:

1. Over medium heat oil in a 4 quart saucepan. Add pepper and carrot, stir occasionally and cook until tender. Add mushrooms, stir and cook for a minute. Add the cayenne pepper and ginger, stir and cook for 30 seconds.

2. Add coconut milk and broth and bring to boil. Regulate the heat to medium. Cook for about 5 minutes. Add chicken, stir and cook until hot.

3. Remove saucepan from the heat

4. Add lime zest, lemon zest and lemon juice, and stir. Add salt to taste.

5. Just before serving, add cilantro

Roasted Asparagus Soup

(Ready in 43 minutes with 15 minutes preparation time- serves 6)

Ingredients:

- 2 pounds of trimmed asparagus spears

- 6 cups of vegetable broth

- 3 tablespoons coconut oil

- 3 tablespoons of all-purpose flour

- 1 large coarsely chopped sweet onion

- 3 minced gloves of garlic

- ½ cup organic milk cream

Cooking directions:

1. Preheat the oven to 425 degrees F

2. On a rimmed baking sheet place the asparagus and sprinkle 1 tablespoon oil

3. Roast the asparagus until tender, about 10 minutes. Leave to cool and chop into small pieces, about 1-inch

4. While roasting the asparagus, Pour the remaining oil in a 4-quart saucepot and heat it over medium heat. Add

garlic and onion, cook until the onions are tender, about 5 minutes.

5. Lower the heat. To the onion mixtures add flour, and cook for about 5 minutes. Add broth and stir gradually. Bring to boil, and cook for about 10 minutes.

6. Add the roasted asparagus to the saucepan

7. Blend the mixture until it is smooth

8. Add organic cream and continue blending, until evenly mixed.

9. Add salt to taste

10. Ready to serve

Garlic-Ginger Beef & Noodle Soup

(Ready in 30 minutes with 10 minutes preparation time- serves 4)

Ingredients:

- 4 Cups of beef broth

- I tablespoon olive oil

- 1 pound minced beef top sirloin steak

- ½ cup minced garlic

- 3 teaspoons of fresh ginger, minced

- 4 ounces, broken into thirds thin spaghetti noodles, uncooked

- I package stir-fry vegetable blend, frozen

- 1 tablespoon soy sauce

Cooking directions:

1. In a large bowl mix 2 teaspoons ginger, 1 tablespoon garlic, olive oil, and beef; toss to coat. Marinate it in refrigerate while covered, for about 30 minutes to 2 hours.

2. In a large pan combine broth with the remaining ginger, garlic and heat to boil. Add pasta and vegetables, stir and boil. Reduce the heat. Keep the pan uncovered, until the vegetables and pasta are tender, about 6 minutes. Remember to stir occasionally.

3. In the meantime, over a medium-high heat, heat a large nonstick skillet until hot. Add the remaining beef, fry and stir until the pink color disappears. Remove the skillet and repeat the same process on the other half. Set it aside and keep warm.

4. Remove the soup from heat, and add beef. Season with soy sauce.

5. Ready to serve

Green Potato Soup

(Ready in 45 minutes with 10 minutes preparation time- serves 4)

Ingredients:

- 5 cups chicken broth

- 2 pounds potatoes, peeled and cubed

- 1 pound hot Italian sausage, cubed

- 2 teaspoon pepper

- ½ cup organic milk cream

- 1 pound shredded fresh spinach

- 1/8 teaspoon pepper

Cooking directions:

1. Bring ½ of broth and potatoes to boil. Reduce heat, cover and simmer for about 20 minutes. Cook until the potatoes are tender. Mash the cooked potatoes

2. While potatoes are cooking, fry-drain sausages on paper towels

3. Add the reaming broth on the mash potatoes, heat and bring to boil. Add greens, cook for about 5 minutes or

until wilted. Add peeper, sausage, cream and salt. Stir gently

4. Heat and serve

Turkey Zoodle Soup

(Ready in 45 minutes with 20 minutes preparation time- serves 6)

Ingredients:

- 3 cloves minced garlic

- 3 zucchini squash, make noodles using a spiralizer

- 1 cup carrots, sliced

- Salt and pepper to taste

- 350 g leftover turkey cut into bite-size cubes

- ½ teaspoon dried oregano

- ½ teaspoon dried basil

- 2 tablespoons sliced celery

- 2 tablespoons cooking oil

- Chicken broth

- ¼ cup thyme

Cooking directions:

1. Over medium heat, heat oil in a large skillet and then sauté the celery, onion, and garlic until all the

ingredients are tender, this should take about 5 minutes.

2. Into the pot, add the chicken broth, salt and pepper, turkey, carrots, thyme, oregano and basil and cook for about 20 minutes ensuring that the vegetables get tender.

3. Put the zucchini noodles into soup bowls and then pour in the cooked mixture over them and serve.

Spicy Sausage & Kale Soup

(Ready in 35 minutes with 10 minutes preparation time- serves 4)

Ingredients:

- 350 g decased sausage

- 1 teaspoon red pepper flakes

- 2 garlic minced garlic cloves

- 1 large peeled and spiralized carrot, Blade D

- ½ cup diced onions

- 1 teaspoon dried oregano

- 4 cups chopped curly kale

- 6 cups low sodium chicken broth

- Salt and pepper

- ¼ cup Romano cheese

Cooking directions:

1. Cook sausage in a large saucepan over medium heat for about 15 minutes crumbling as you cook.

2. After adding the salt, pepper, onions, and garlic, cook for another 3 minutes ensuring that the onions start to soften.

3. Cook for another minute after adding the kale

4. Add the oregano and broth and cook on high heat so that it starts to boil. When it starts boiling, add the carrot and combine by stirring.

5. Turn down the heat to low and cook for another 5 minutes ensuring that the carrot is cooked through.

6. Garnish with cheese and red pepper flacks before serving.

Ginger Tofu & Green Tea Soup

(Ready in 15 minutes with 10 minutes preparation time- serves 4)

Ingredients:

- 1 ½ cups water

- Pepper to taste

- 2 green tea bags

- 1 ½ medium zucchinis Blade C

- 1 teaspoon sesame oil

- 1 teaspoon soy sauce

- ½ teaspoon minced ginger

- 1/3 cup chopped scallions

- 1 ½ cup vegetable broth

- 1 tablespoon miso paste

- ½ cup small diced tofu

Cooking directions:

1. Boil water in a medium saucepan, and then remove
   from the heat before you add the tea bags and allow to

steep for 3 to 4 minutes. Remove the tea bags from the water and set both aside.

2. In a medium saucepan placed over medium heat, add the sesame oil before adding the ginger and allow to cook for just about 30 seconds.

3. Pour the tofu, vegetable stock, and green tea and get to boil.

4. Scoop out about 1/3 cup of the soup and pour into a bowl, before you add in the miso paste and get it dissolved in.

5. Pour the miso broth in the saucepan and reduce the amount of heat.

6. Add the pepper, soy source, zucchini noodles, and scallions and leave to cook for about 3 minutes ensuring that the zucchini softens.

7. Serve the soup.

Mexican Sweet Potato Soup with Avocado

(Ready in 15 minutes with 15 minutes preparation time- serves 2)

Ingredients:

- 1 tablespoon cooking oil

- 1 cubed avocado

- 1 garlic clove

- 1 ½ tablespoons chopped cilantro

- ½ diced yellow onion

- 1 peeled large sweet potato, Blade C

- 1 can diced tomatoes, 400g

- 3 cups vegetable broth

- ½ teaspoon ground coriander

- 1 tablespoon chili powder

Cooking directions:

1. Cook the garlic in a large saucepan with heated cooking oil for 30 seconds and the put in the onion and leave to cook for another 2 minutes.

2. Add the diced tomatoes, pepper, salt, coriander, and chili and cook for another 3 minutes before adding the chicken broth and sweet potatoes and then reducing to simmer.

3. Cook for another 5 or so minutes until the sweet potatoes reach a consistency you are happy with. Toss in the cilantro when you are halfway through the cooking.

4. Fold in the avocado when the soup is done.

5. Transfer into serving bowls and then garnish with the cilantro that remains.

Hungarian Sausage and Spinach Soup
(Ready in 25 minutes with 10 minutes preparation time- serves 6)

Ingredients:

- 3 pcs. Hungarian Sausage, chopped into small bits
- 1 tbsp. butter
- 1 onion, diced
- 1 carrot, diced
- 2 cloves garlic, minced
- 2 tbsp. apple cider vinegar
- 1 tsp. oregano powder
- 1 tsp. basil, dried
- 1 tsp. sage, dried
- 4 c. vegan broth
- 1 c. heavy cream
- 1 c. cauliflower florets
- 3 c. spinach leaves, chopped
- ¼ tsp. red pepper flakes
- Salt and pepper to taste

Cooking directions:

1. Using a casserole, brown the Hungarian sausage. Let the natural oil sweat out. Remove the cooked Hungarian sausage and set aside a plate lined with paper towels. Throw away the drippings.

2. Using the same casserole, melt the butter over low-medium heat. Add in the onion and carrot. Cook until the carrots are a bit tender.

3. Add in the garlic and vinegar. Don't worry if the bottom of the casserole is browning a bit. Just scrape the bottom of the casserole every minute or so.

4. Add in the dried herbs and pepper flakes. After a few seconds, add in the stock and cream. Increase the heat to high. Let this boil. Once it boils, add in the cauliflower and then turn down the heat to medium. Let the soup simmer without the cover.

5. After 10 minutes, throw in the spinach leaves and sausage. Cook for another 3 minutes.

6. Finally season with salt and pepper.

7. Serve and enjoy.

Potato Soup

(Ready in 1 hour with 20 minutes preparation time- serves 6)

Ingredients:

- 6 large baking potatoes peeled and cubed
- 6 slices cooked bacon
- 1 cup Cheddar cheeses shredded
- ½ tsp salt (each potato)
- ½ tsp pepper (each potato)
- 2 cups whipping cream
- 2 onions chopped
- 3 tbs flour

Cooking directions:

1. Boil potatoes until tender
2. Drain and set aside
3. In separate pot, combine cream, salt, pepper, and flour
4. Stir until thickened, add cheese, stir
5. Add potatoes, keep warm until serving

Creamy Cauliflower Soup
(Ready in 35 minutes with 10 minutes preparation time- serves 6)

Ingredients:

- 1 quart chicken broth
- 1 diced onion
- ½ cup butter
- ¾ cup celery
- 1 cup chopped carrot
- 3 garlic cloves
- 1 tsp parsley
- 1 cauliflower
- 1 cup of milk
- 1 cup of sour cream
- 8 ounces of cheese (grated)
- Chives
- 12 slices of chopped and cooked bacon
- 2 tsp of garlic powder
- Salt and pepper

Cooking directions:

1. Start by melting the butter and put the pot to sauté setting.

2. Add carrot, onion, garlic, and celery to it and cook for 5-6 minutes.

3. When the veggies are tender, add cauliflower, chicken broth and parsley.

4. Lock the pressure cooker and heat it for another 3 minutes at Low Pressure.

5. Meanwhile, melt butter and whisk some flour to form a paste.

6. Add milk to the mixture and continue whisking it.

7. Sprinkle the desired quantity of salt, pepper and garlic powder.

8. Simmer the cooker and add the whisked contents to it.

9. Add cheese and sour cream and let it simmer for another few minutes. Sprinkle the sour with some bacon, chives and extra cheese before serving it hot.

Easy Pot Mushroom Soup

(Ready in 35 minutes with 10 minutes preparation time- serves 6)

Ingredients:

- 8 oz. white mushrooms
- ¼ cup of milk
- 2 tbsp of virgin oil
- 2 cups of water
- ¼ cup of chicken broth
- 4 tbsp butter
- 4 tbsp flour

Cooking directions:

1. Add oil and sliced mushrooms to the pot to sauté them until they become tender and darker.

2. Add chicken broth to the mix.

3. Put it to the Pressurize mode and set it to quick release feature. Drain the mushrooms while saving the broth.

4. Place the mushrooms back in the pot. Add butter to it and let them simmer.

5. Add flour to the mix and stir it gently.

6. Lastly, add the mushroom broth and let it all dissolve to give a smooth texture.

7. Whisk it for another 8 minutes and add milk to it to complete the recipe.

Vegan Vietnamese Pho

(Ready in 30 minutes with 10 minutes preparation time- serves 4)

Ingredients:

- 6 oz. flat rice noodles

- 3 c. homemade vegan broth*

- 2 tbsp. light soy sauce

- 1 small cinnamon bark

- 1 knob ginger, thinly sliced

- 2 pcs. star anise

- 4 oz. tofu cubes

- ¼ c. green onions, cut into short strips

- 2 c. bokchoy, shredded

- ½ c. lemon basil, fresh

Cooking directions:

1. Cook noodles by following the instructions on package. Drain and set aside.

2. In a stock pot, heat the vegan broth, cinnamon, light soy sauce, ginger, and star anise. Once the mixture

boils, reduce heat and cover. Simmer for another 10 minutes.

3. Add the tofu cubes and green onions to the hot broth. Simmer for another 5 minutes.

4. Remove the star anise and cinnamon bark.

5. In a soup bowl, put ¼ of the cooked noodles. Add the broth while still hot. Top the soup with shredded bokchoy and lemon basil.

* *Ingredients for Vegan Broth:*

> - 2 large white onion, peeled
> - 2 large carrot, peeled cut in half
> - 5 cloves garlic, peeled
> - 2 stalk celery, cut in big strips
> - 4 c. water
> - Salt and pepper to taste

(Put all these in a stock pot and boil for 10 minutes. Remove all floating impurities.)

Hearty Italian Minestrone

(Ready in 30 minutes with 10 minutes preparation time- serves 4)

Ingredients:

- 3 c. homemade vegan broth

- ½ c. tomato sauce

- 1 c. green beans, frozen

- 1 carrot, cubed

- 1 small potato, cubed

- ½ can diced tomatoes

- 1 small onion, chopped

- ½ c. whole kernel corn, frozen

- 1 celery stalk, chopped

- 1 tbsp. Italian seasoning

- ¼ tsp. ground black pepper

- 1 c. croutons

Cooking directions:

1. In a soup casserole, boil the vegan broth sprinkled with black pepper and Italian seasoning.

2. As soon as the seasoned broth boils, add the green beans, corn, carrots, diced tomatoes, potato, onion, and celery. Bring it to a boil. Cover the casserole, reduce heat, and simmer for another 15 minutes.

3. Finally, add the tomato sauce. Simmer for another 5 minutes

4. Serve in soup bowls and top with croutons.

Mexican Tortilla Soup

(Ready in 40 minutes with 10 minutes preparation time- serves 2)

Ingredients:

- 1 tbsp. coconut oil

- 1 oz. cooked black beans, drained

- 1 oz. whole kernel corn, drained

- ½ c. onion, chopped

- 1 clove garlic, minced

- ¼ c. red pepper, chopped

- ½ c. red salsa, chunky

- 2 c. homemade vegan broth

- 1 tbsp. maple syrup

- ¼ tsp. cumin

- ¼ tsp. chili powder

- Salt and pepper to taste

- 1 bunch coriander, fresh

- Lime wedges

- 1 tortilla, cut in strips

- ½ c. avocado, cubed

Cooking directions:

1. In a large saucepan, heat the coconut oil. Sauté the garlic and onions. Add the red pepper. Season with cumin, chili powder, salt and pepper. Sauté for a couple of minutes until vegetables have released flavors.

2. Add in the red salsa. Infuse the salsa with the flavors and then add the broth and maple syrup. Stir continuously until mixture boils.

3. Add the corn and beans. Stir and bring mixture to a boil. Cover, reduce heat, and simmer for 20 minutes. Stir the mixture every few minutes.

4. Serve in a bowl and top with tortilla strips, coriander leaves, avocado, and lime wedge.

Veggie Barley Soup

(Ready in 40 minutes with 10 minutes preparation time- serves 4)

Ingredients:

- 1 c. frozen mixed vegetables
- ¼ c. onions, chopped
- ½ c. celery, chopped
- ¼ c. pearl barley
- ½ can diced tomatoes
- 3 c. homemade vegan broth
- ½ c. packed vegan burger, chopped
- Salt and pepper to taste

Cooking directions:

1. In a soup casserole, boil broth and mixed vegetables. Add the onions, celery, barley, and diced tomatoes.

2. As soon as mixture boils, add the chopped vegan burgers, salt and pepper. Bring it to a boil again.

3. Cover, reduce heat, and simmer for 30 minutes.

4. Serve in a soup bowl.

Healthy Lentil Soup
(Ready in 30 minutes with 10 minutes preparation time- serves 4)

Ingredients:

- 2 tbsp. olive oil

- 1 c. carrots, diced

- ½ c. onions, diced

- ¼ c. red bell pepper, diced

- 1 c. potato, diced

- 1 clove garlic, pounded

- 2 Roma tomatoes, peeled and diced

- 1 bay leaf

- 1 c. Spanish lentils

- 5 c. homemade vegan broth

Cooking directions:

1. In a large casserole, heat the olive oil over low heat. Sauté the onions and garlic. Once the onions are translucent, add the carrots. After a couple of minutes add the potato and then finally the red bell pepper. Increase the heat to medium and wait for the

vegetables to soften. Stir frequently to avoid burning the vegetables.

2. Reduce the heat to low again and then add in the tomatoes, lentils, and bay leaf.

3. Add the broth and bring to a boil. Cover, reduce heat, and simmer for 20 minutes or until the lentils are perfectly cooked.

4. Season the soup with salt and pepper.

5. Serve in a soup bowl with a side of bread sticks.

Special Slow Cooker Hot and Sour Soup

(Ready in 7 hours with 10 minutes preparation time- serves 5)

Ingredients:

- 2 c. fresh bamboo shoots, cut into thin strips

- 2 skinless chicken breast, ground

- 1 pack tofu, cubed

- 1 large carrot, peeled and cut into thin strips

- 2 stalks leeks, cut into strips

- 4 c. chicken stock

- ¼ c. Chinese rice wine

- ¼ c. light soy sauce

- 1 knob ginger, grated

- 3 cloves garlic, grated

- 1 tbsp. hot sauce

- ¼ c. water

- 2 tbps. cornstarch

- Salt and pepper to taste

Cooking directions:

1. Place all ingredients in the slow cooker but leave out the tofu, cornstarch, and water. Cook over low heat for six hours.

2. While waiting, mix the water and cornstarch. Set aside.

3. Add the corn starch mix and tofu to the soup after 6 hours. Cook for another hour.

4. Serve and enjoy.

Tasty Slow Cooker Turkey Tortilla Soup

(Ready in 8 hours with 10 minutes preparation time- serves 4)

Ingredients:

- ½ kilo bone-in turkey breast

- 1 red onion, diced

- ½ red bell pepper, seeded and diced

- 2 cloves garlic, minced

- ½ c. beef stock

- 1 can whole peeled tomatoes

- 1 c. tomato sauce

- 1 small can green chiles, chopped

- 1 tsp. red pepper flakes

- 1 tsp. oregano powder

- ½ tsp. cumin powder

- ½ pack frozen yellow squash, sliced

- ½ c. green beans, sliced

- 1 juice of lime

- ¼ c. fresh coriander, chopped

- Salt and pepper to taste

- Sour cream and toasted tortilla as siding

Cooking directions:

1. In a slow cooker, mix the turkey breasts, onion, bell pepper, garlic, beef stock, tomatoes, tomato sauce, green chiles, red pepper flakes, oregano, and cumin. Sprinkle over some salt and pepper. Cook on low heat for 7 hours or until turkey breasts are tender.

2. Add the thawed sliced yellow squash and green beans. Cook for another hour.

3. Before serving, remove the turkey bones and add the lime juice.

4. Serve with a dollop of sour cream and a side of toasted tortilla.

Sopa de Ajo (Slow Cooker Garlic Soup)

(Ready in 8 hours with 10 minutes preparation time- serves 6)

Ingredients:

- ¼ c. olive oil

- 1 white onion, diced

- 4 bulbs garlic, peeled and separated in cloves

- 6 c. vegetable broth

- 1 lemon, juice

- 1 tomato, diced

- 1 c. feta cheese

- 1 c. croutons

- 2 stalks green onions, chopped

- Salt and pepper to taste

Cooking directions:

1. Combine the oil, onion, and garlic in the slow cooker, cook these on low for 5 hours.

2. Add in the vegetable broth and cook for a couple more hours.

3. Transfer the mixture to a blender and pulse until smooth. Place back into the slow cooker. Add the lemon juice, salt, and pepper.

4. Serve in a bowl topped with tomatoes, feta cheese, and croutons.

Slow Cooker Caribbean Black Bean Soup

(Ready in 6 hours with 10 minutes preparation time- serves 4)

Ingredients:

- ½ kilo black bean, washed and drained
- 2 red onions, diced
- 1 large carrot, peeled and diced
- 1 c. diced fire roasted tomatoes
- 1 c. crushed tomatoes
- 1 Caribbean pepper, seeded and chopped
- 1 yellow capsicum, cored, seeded, and chopped
- 1 red bell pepper, cored, seeded, and chopped
- 1 sprig cilantro, chopped
- 1 ½ tbsp. cumin powder
- 1 tsp. cayenne powder
- ½ tsp. Sriracha
- 4 cloves garlic, minced
- 1 bay leaf
- 6 c. chicken broth
- 2 c. water

- Sea salt and pepper to taste

Cooking directions:

1. Place the washed black bean in a basin and soak with 2 cups of water overnight.

2. Drain and rinse the black beans. Combine the beans with tomatoes, garlic, onion, chicken stock, salt, pepper, cumin, cayenne, sriracha, bay leaf, and Caribbean pepper in the slow cooker. Cover over high heat for 4 hours.

3. Add the carrots, cilantro, capsicum, and bell pepper. Season with salt and pepper again. Put the heat to low and cook for 2 hours.

4. Serve in a bowl with a dollop of sour cream.

Slow Cooker Pumpkin and Peanut Soup

(Ready in 6 hours with 10 minutes preparation time- serves 4)

Ingredients:

- 500 g. pumpkin, peeled and cubed
- 1 tbsp. olive oil
- 1 white onion, diced
- 2 cloves garlic, minced
- 3 c. vegetable broth
- 3 pcs. Serrano chili, chopped
- 1 small knob ginger, minced
- 1 tsp. allspice powder
- 1 c. tomato juice
- ½ c. organic peanut butter
- Salt and pepper to taste
- Fresh parsley for garnish

Cooking directions:

1. Sauté the garlic, onions, and ginger in a non-stick pan. After a couple of minutes, turn off the heat.

2. Place all the ingredients, including the sautéed vegetables, in a slow cooker. Cook over low heat for 6 hours.

3. Transfer the coarse soup to a blend, a batch at a time. Whiz until it turns into a smooth mixture.

4. Serve in a bowl topped with chopped parsley.

Slow Cooker Bean and Vegetable Clear Soup

(Ready in 5 hours with 10 minutes preparation time- serves 4)

Ingredients:

- ½ kilo dry white beans
- 2 stalks celery, chopped
- 1 c. broccoli florets, chopped
- 1 red onion, chopped
- 4 cloves garlic, minced
- 2 large carrots, peeled and diced
- 1 tsp. fennel seeds
- 2 tsp. oregano powder
- ¼ tsp. red pepper flakes
- 5 c. vegan broth
- Salt and pepper to taste

Cooking directions:

1. Place all the ingredients in a slow cooker. Cook on high for 5 hours. Check if the beans are already tender before serving.

2. Serve in individual bowls. Enjoy.

Slow Cooker Yummy Corn Chowder
(Ready in 7 hours with 10 minutes preparation time- serves 5)

Ingredients:

- 2 tbsp. corn oil

- 1 large white onion, coarsely chopped

- 1 large red bell pepper, cored and diced

- 2 large russet potatoes, peeled and diced

- 2 cans sweet corn kernels with brine

- 2 ½ c. vegan broth

- 1 tsp. cumin powder

- ½ tsp. Spanish paprika

- 1 c. almond milk

- Salt and pepper to taste

- Chopped green onions for garnish

Cooking directions:

1. Sauté the onions in corn oil until it turns translucent. Transfer onions to slow cooker.

2. Add all the ingredients, except for the green onions, in the slow cooker.

3. Cook on low for 7 hours.

4. Transfer the soup to a blender and pulse until it forms a smooth chowder.

5. Serve and enjoy.

Hearty Slow Cooker Mung Bean Soup

(Ready in 9 hours with 10 minutes preparation time- serves 5)

Ingredients:

- ½ kilo yellow mung beans, washed and drained
- 2 stalks celery, chopped
- 6 stalks green onions, chopped
- 2 large carrots, peeled and diced
- 2 cloves garlic, minced
- 1 red onion, diced
- 6 c. vegan broth
- 1 bay leaf
- Salt and pepper to taste
- 2 tbsp. sesame oil for serving

Cooking directions:

1. Combine all the ingredients in a slow cook. Cook on low heat for 9 hours or until the beans are tender.

2. Place in individual bowls. Drizzle over sesame oil before serving.

Slow Cooker Taro Soup

(Ready in 5 hours with 10 minutes preparation time- serves 5)

Ingredients:

- 1 kilo fresh taro, peeled, washed and cubed
- 1 white onion, diced
- 4 cloves garlic, minced
- 2 stalks celery, chopped
- 5 c. vegan broth
- 1 c. almond milk
- 1 tsp. tarragon leaves
- 2 c. water cress
- Salt and pepper to taste
- ½ c. toasted slivered almonds, for garnish

Cooking directions:

1. Combine the vegan broth, taro, onions, celery, and garlic in a slow cooker. Cook on high heat for 5 hours or until taro is tender.

2. If taro is tender, turn off heat. Pour in the milk and add the seasonings. Mix well.

3. Transfer the soup to a blender and whiz until smooth.

4. Transfer to a large bowl. While the soup is piping hot, add the water cress. Stir gently.

5. Serve in individual bowls topped with almonds. Enjoy.

Vegetarian Slow Cooker Rigatoni Soup

(Ready in 7 hours with 10 minutes preparation time- serves 5)

Ingredients:

- 1 white onion, diced
- 1 c. fresh button mushrooms, halved
- 1 zucchini, peeled and diced
- 2 cloves garlic, minced
- ½ c. tomato sauce
- 1 c. diced tomatoes, in can
- 3 c. vegan broth
- 1 bay leaf
- 1 tsp. oregano powder
- ½ tbsp. dried basil leaves
- 2 c. fresh kale leaves
- 200 g. rigatoni noodles (cooked according to package instructions)
- Salt and pepper to taste
- Fresh basil leaves for garnish

Cooking directions:

1. Place all ingredients, except for the garnish and pasta, in a slow cooker. Cook on low heat for 7 hours.

2. After 6 ½ hours, cook the rigatoni noodles in a medium casserole according to package instructions.

3. Add the noodles to the soup after the timer's done.

4. Serve in individual bowls topped with fresh basil leaves

Slow Cooker Red Bean Soup

(Ready in 11 hours with 10 minutes preparation time- serves 5)

Ingredients:

- ½ kilo dry red beans, washed and soaked in water for 5 hours

- 1 white onion, diced

- 1 red bell pepper, cored and diced

- 4 c. vegan broth

- 3 cloves garlic, minced

- 1 bay leaf

- ½ tbsp. cumin powder

- Salt and pepper to taste

- Chopped fresh coriander for garnish

Cooking directions:

1. Place all the ingredients, except for the coriander, in a slow cooker. Cook over low heat for 11 hours or until the red beans are tender.

2. Transfer the soup in a blender and pulse until it turns smooth.

3. Serve in individual bowls topped with chopped coriander.

Slow Cooker Vegetarian Minestrone

(Ready in 7 hours with 10 minutes preparation time- serves 8)

Ingredients:

- 1 zucchini, cubed

- 1 carrot, cubed

- 2 stalks celery, chopped

- 1 white onion, chopped

- 1 clove garlic, minced

- 2 c. vegetable broth

- 2 c. tomato juice

- ½ c. button mushrooms, drained

- 1 tbsp. dried basil

- ½ tsp. oregano powder

- ½ can diced tomatoes

- 1 c. raw elbow macaroni

- Salt and pepper to taste

- 2 tbsp. pecorino romano cheese, grated

Cooking directions:

1. Place all the ingredients in the slow cooker except for the elbow macaroni and cheese. Cover over low heat for 6 hours.

2. After 6 hours, stir in the pasta. Cook for another 30 minutes over high heat.

3. Serve on a bowl. Sprinkle over the grated cheese.

Pressure Cooker Hubbard Squash with Cumin Soup

(Ready in 35 minutes with 10 minutes preparation time- serves 6)

Ingredients:

- 1 tbsp. palm oil

- 1 white onion, diced

- 2 cloves garlic, minced

- 1 kilo Hubbard squash, peeled and cubed

- ½ tsp. ginger powder

- ½ tsp. cumin powder

- 1 tsp. garam masala

- ¼ tsp. cayenne pepper

- 3 c. vegan broth

- 1 c. yellow mung beans

- 1 can diced tomatoes

- 1 sprig coriander, chopped finely

Cooking directions:

1. Using the instant pot, sauté the onion and garlic in palm oil until the onions turn translucent.

2. Add in the powder spices and the squash. Let the squash take in all the aromas from the spices.

3. After a couple of minutes, add the mung beans and broth. Cover and seal the pot. Cook over high heat for 5 minutes.

4. After 5 minutes, let the mixture stay warm and settle for another 10 minutes.

5. Add in the tomatoes and cook over medium heat for another 5 minutes.

6. Release the pressure and uncover the pot. Transfer the mixture in several batches into a blender. Blend until it forms a creamy soup.

7. Serve in a bowl topped with chopped coriander. Enjoy.

Hearty Pressure Cooker Red Bean Soup

(Ready in 45 minutes with 10 minutes preparation time- serves 8)

Ingredients:

- 1 red onion, diced

- 1 green bell pepper, cored and diced

- 1 red bell pepper, cored and diced

- 1 can crushed tomatoes

- 1 cup celery sticks, diced

- ½ kilo red beans, washed and drained

- 1 tsp. sriracha sauce

- 1 tbsp. smoked paprika

- 1 tsp. red chili powder

- 2 tbsp. cumin powder

- 1 bay leaf

- 6 c. vegan broth

- Sea salt and pepper to taste

- 6 lime wedges (for serving)

- 1 avocado, diced (for serving)

Cooking directions:

1. Place all the ingredients in the instant pot. Cover and seal using the lid. Set the pot on high pressure for 40 minutes. After 40 minutes, let the pressure release itself naturally. Carefully remove the lid and remove the bay leaf.

2. Serve in a bowl with a lime wedge and topped with avocado cubes.

Pressure Cooker Green Mung Bean and Spinach Soup

(Ready in 45 minutes with 10 minutes preparation time- serves 4)

Ingredients:

- 2 tsp. palm oil

- 1 white onion, diced

- 1 large carrots, peeled and diced

- 1 large celery stalk, diced

- 4 cloves garlic, minced

- 2 tsp. cumin powder

- 1 tsp. turmeric powder

- 1 tsp. thyme powder

- 1 c. green mung beans, washed and drained

- 4 c. vegan broth

- 6 c. spinach leaves, washed and drained

- Salt and pepper to taste

Cooking directions:

1. Using the instant pot, sauté the onions, garlic, carrots, and celery in palm oil for 4 minutes. Once the onions and celery turn translucent and tender, respectively, add in the powder spices. Season with salt and pepper. Sauté these for another couple of minutes.

2. Add in the mung beans. Stir the beans well to let the spices coat the seeds.

3. Pour in the broth.

4. Cover the pot and seal. Cook for another 12 minutes using the timer under manual option.

5. After 12 minutes, carefully let the vent release the pressure in the pot. Remove the lid once the vents are completely open.

6. Add in the spinach. Season with salt and pepper if needed.

7. Serve in a bowl. Enjoy.

Pressure Cooker Pinto Beans with Vegetable Soup

(Ready in 45 minutes with 10 minutes preparation time- serves 8)

Ingredients:

- 1 small red onion, diced

- 2 c. broccoli florets, chopped

- 1 carrots, peeled and cubed

- 1 sugar beet, peeled and cubed

- 3 red potatoes, peeled and cubed

- 8 c. vegan broth

- 1 can pinto beans, drained

- Salt and pepper to taste

Cooking directions:

1. Place all the ingredients in an Instant Pot. Close and seal the lid. Cook over high heat for 30 minutes.

2. After 30 minutes, wait for the pressure to release naturally.

3. Serve in a bowl. Enjoy.

Pressure Cooker Carrots and Turnips Soup

(Ready in 30 minutes with 10 minutes preparation time- serves 4)

Ingredients:

- 1 tbsp. olive oil

- 1 white onion, coarsely chopped

- 3 carrots, peeled and diced

- 2 turnips, peeled and diced

- 1 ½ c. broccoli florets, chopped

- 15 pcs. asparagus, chopped

- 6 c. vegan broth

- Salt and pepper to taste

Cooking directions:

1. Sauté the onion in the Instant Pot until it turns translucent. Add the carrots, turnips, asparagus, and broccoli. Stir constantly. Pour in the stock.

2. Cover and seal the lid. Set to manual and cook for 10 minutes.

3. After 10 minutes, allow the steam to naturally release. Remove the lid. Transfer the vegetable mix to a blender and puree.

4. Serve in a bowl. Enjoy.

Mediterranean Pressure Cooker Vegetable Soup

(Ready in 35 minutes with 10 minutes preparation time- serves 4)

Ingredients:

- 3 tbsp. olive oil

- 1 red onion, diced

- 1 clove garlic, minced

- 3 c. Napa cabbage, washed, drained, and finely chopped

- 2 carrots, peeled and cubed

- 2 stalks celery, chopped

- 1 can Great Northern Beans, drained

- 4 c. vegan broth

- 1 can fire-roasted tomatoes

- Salt and pepper to taste

- 2 sprigs parsley, chopped (for topping)

Cooking directions:

1. Set the Instant Pot to saute and heat the oil. Place the onions and saute until it turns translucent. Constantly stir to avoid burning it.

2. Add the garlic and Napa cabbage and cook for another 4 minutes.

3. Once the cabbage softens, add the carrots, beans, and celery. Season with salt and pepper. Constantly stir the vegetables.

4. After 5 minutes, add the vegan broth and tomatoes.

5. Cover the pot and seal the lid. Set to "Soup" mode and cook for 10 minutes.

6. After 10 minutes, wait for the pressure to naturally release before removing the lid.

7. Serve in a bowl topped with chopped parsley.

Quick-Cook Pressure Cooker Tomato Soup

(Ready in 20 minutes with 5 minutes preparation time- serves 4)

Ingredients:

- 1 red onion, diced
- 1 tbsp. canola oil
- 2 tbsp. tomato paste
- 2 large cans diced tomatoes
- 3 c. vegan broth
- 2 tsp. dried parsley
- 3 tsp. dried basil
- 1 tbsp. apple cider vinegar
- 1 tbsp. red wine
- ¼ c. granulated sugar
- Salt and pepper to taste
- Handful of fresh basil leaves (for topping)

Cooking directions:

1. Press "Sauté" and heat the oil. Sauté the onion until it softens. Add the tomato paste and constantly stir the mix.

2. Press the "Cancel" button and press "Soup."

3. Add the tomatoes and vegan broth. Stir to make sure the ingredients are mixed well and nothing sticks to the bottom.

4. Season the soup with the spices. Cover and seal the lid and cook for 10 minutes.

5. After 10 minutes, let the Instant Pot naturally release the steam. Open the lid.

6. Add the cider vinegar, wine, and sugar. Stir well.

7. Transfer the soup to a blender and puree. Season with salt and pepper if needed.

8. Serve in a bowl topped with fresh basil leaves.

Pressure Cooker Spanish Lentil and Sausage Soup

(Ready in 20 minutes with 5 minutes preparation time- serves 6)

Ingredients:

- 1 liter of water

- 400 grams of lentils

- 1/2 Spanish chorizo, sliced 1 cm

- 1 potato, peeled and chopped

- 2 carrots, chopped

- 1 bay leaf

- 75 milliliters of extra virgin olive oil

- 1 onion, chopped

- 2 teaspoons paprika

Cooking directions:

1. Place water in a pressure cooker then add lentils, chorizo, potatoes, carrot and bay leaf. Cover and cook 10 minutes from the moment the valve starts ringing.

2. Meanwhile, heat the olive oil in a frying pan over medium heat. Add onion and sauté until it looks

transparent, about 5 minutes. Add the paprika and mix well. Remove from heat to prevent burning paprika.

3. Add the onion with oil lentil soup. Mix well and serve.

Pressure Cooker Chilled Fruit Soup

(Ready in 10 minutes with 5 minutes preparation time- serves 4)

Ingredients:

- 1 tbsp of powdered sugar

- 2 peaches (remove the pit)

- ½ cantaloupes

- 8 oz of Greek yogurt

- 16 oz of fresh pineapple juice

- 1 large sized orange (cut it in two halves each)

- 1 tbsp of chia seeds

- ½ tsp of vanilla

Cooking directions:

1. Take the prepared fruit having the pineapple juice

2. Add it to the pressure cooker tactfully.

3. Put the pressure to HP for the next 5 minutes and release it quickly after that.

4. Now, pour it in a blender after the time is up and puree it until the texture becomes smooth.

5. Pour it using a strainer.

6. Let it cool to room temperature and now add vanilla, powdered sugar and some Greek yogurt.

7. Whisk to mix thoroughly.

8. Chill and serve with chia seeds for best results.

Pressure Cooker Chicken Noodle Soup

(Ready in 20 minutes with 5 minutes preparation time- serves 5)

Ingredients:

- 4 large carrots

- 2 cups of diced chicken

- 6 cups of chicken stock

- 1 onion (diced)

- Egg noodles

- 1 diced celery rib

- 1 tbsp of butter

- Salt and pepper

Cooking directions:

1. Take the lid off from the pressure pot and select sauté mode before adding anything.

2. When the butter has been melted, add some onion and cook it for 1 to 2 minutes.

3. Now, you can add carrots and celery as well. Let them sauté for nearly 5 minutes.

4. This would be your cue to add chicken stock and chicken.

5. Place the pot to HP and set the timer for 5 minutes.

6. After that wait for another 5 minutes for a quick pressure release.

7. Add required salt and pepper.

8. Serve along with prepared noodles.

Pressure Cooker Vegetable Barley Soup

(Ready in 20 minutes with 5 minutes preparation time- serves 6)

Ingredients:

- 1 tsp of olive oil
- 2 garlic cloves
- 1 onion
- ½ cup barley
- 1 carrot
- 1 celery stalk
- 1 bay leaf
- A handful of mushrooms
- 1 large potato
- 4 cups of vegetable stock
- 1 tsp of pounded black pepper
- Salt and pepper

Cooking directions:

1. Start by soaking the barley for around 6 hours before you begin.

2. Make sure that the barley is cooked properly. You can also use a sauce pan method to do so.

3. Turn the pressure cooker on and add garlic, onions and celery to sauté it for the next few minutes. Except for parsley, add the remaining ingredients to it.

4. Now, cover the cooker and heat it for at least the next 10 minutes.

5. Release the pressure naturally.

6. Serve the barley vegetable soup by adding salt and pepper to it.

Pressure Cooker Tortellini Soup

(Ready in 35 minutes with 10 minutes preparation time- serves 6)

Ingredients:

- 1 tbsp dried onions
- 1 tbsp minced garlic
- ½ tbsp of ground pepper
- 1 tbsp of chicken base
- 1 tbsp of dried shallots
- 2 carrots
- ¼ cup of dry vermouth
- 6 ounces of baby spinach
- 6 ounces of cheese tortellini
- 6 cups of chicken stock or broth
- Parmesan cheese

Cooking directions:

1. Add onion, garlic, chicken base, ground pepper, and shallots to the pot.

2. Cut carrots in ¼ inch thick coins and place them in the pot.

3. Place tortellini and add chicken broth and vermouth to it.

4. Set the cooker on High Pressure for 2 minutes with Quick Release.

5. Let the soup cook. Meanwhile, clean spinach leaves.

6. Release the pressure and wait for a few minutes to let the soup settle. Garnish it with parmesan before serving.

Italian Pressure Cooker Chicken Soup

(Ready in 25 minutes with 10 minutes preparation time- serves 6)

Ingredients:

- 2 tsp olive oil
- ½ pound turkey sausage
- 1 large onion chopped
- 2 cloves garlic minced
- 1 cup spinach leaves chopped
- 3 boneless skinless chicken breasts, chopped
- 1/3 cup parsley flakes
- 1 15 ounces can chickpeas
- 1 cup medium salsa
- 3-1/2 cups chicken broth or stock

Cooking directions:

1. Add oil ice oil and heat in cooker
2. Place sausage and chicken in and heat 2 minutes
3. Add onion, garlic, spinach leaves, chickpeas and parsley flakes
4. Add in salsa and stir

5. Pour in chicken broth/stock and stir lightly

6. Cook on high for 20 minutes

7. Use slow release method

Pressure Cooker Pumpkin Soup

(Ready in 15 minutes with 5 minutes preparation time- serves 6)

Ingredients:

- 2 cups canned pumpkin

- 1 cup milk

- 4 cups chicken broth

- 1 cup applesauce

- 1 cinnamon stick

- 1 tsp nutmeg

- 1 tsp ginger

- 1 tsp salt

- ½ tsp pepper

- 1 large Apple, peeled and cut into cubes

Cooking directions:

1. Put pumpkin in cooker, add milk

2. Pour in chicken broth, applesauce, and apple chunks

3. Add salt, pepper, and butter

4. Add ginger and nutmeg, stir

5. Cook on high for 15 minutes, use slow release method

Conclusion

Thank you for taking the time to read the entire cookbook from cover to cover. However, reading is not enough to change your eating habits and your lifestyle in general; it is now time for you to try the recipes listed in this book. Start with what you think is easiest to prepare and more enjoyable to eat with your friends or family. Revolutionize your kitchen by adding a pressure cooker or a slow cooker, if you have the extra budget, so you can explore your kitchen skills with the assistance of this book. The more time you spend in your kitchen, the more time you dedicate for your family and their proper nutrition.

Soups are essential to keep one's health always on the top of the bar. And although you or your family is not yet used to the idea of having soup at the start of the meal or even having it as the center of the meal, it is better to introduce this sooner rather than later. Expect a full 180° change, a positive change at that, with your family's health and energy. By just adding this one, important dish in your menu, you actually prevent many things – illnesses, extra trips to the doctor, and extra expenses for medicines. Imagine that!

So what are you waiting for? Start your soup journey and take your family to wonderful dining experiences as you share a casserole of soup. Share joyous daily goings-on and get to know one another better as you partake of the dishes served on the dining table. The best conversations are shared while breaking bread and how else to perfectly start it with a bowl of warm, soothing soup that creates the perfect ambience in the home. Broaden your scope of influence by inviting over close friends and families and re-introduce to them the importance of soup dishes during meal times. There is no limit to what you can do when it comes to the improvement of the family's diet and nutrition.

27146207R00055

Printed in Great Britain
by Amazon